The Time Machine

by H. G. Wells

Abridged and adapted by T. Ernesto Bethancourt
Illustrated by James McConnell

A PACEMAKER CLASSIC

Fearon Education
a division of
David S. Lake Publishers
Belmont, California

Pacemaker Classics

The Adventures of Tom Sawyer
The Deerslayer
Dr. Jekyll and Mr. Hyde
Frankenstein
Great Expectations
Jane Eyre
The Jungle Book
The Last of the Mohicans
The Moonstone
Robinson Crusoe
A Tale of Two Cities
The Three Musketeers
The Time Machine
Treasure Island
20,000 Leagues Under the Sea
Two Years Before the Mast

Library of Congress Catalog Card Number: 84-61434

ISBN-0-8224-9256-3

Printed in the United States of America

1. 9 8 7 6 5 4 3

Contents

Introduction

How many times have you thought about what life will be like a hundred or a thousand years from now? Many movies and books show the future in different ways. But H. G. Wells was the first person to write a book about traveling into the future.

Wells was born in England in 1866. He wrote *The Time Machine* in 1895—almost a hundred years ago. At that time, life was very hard for workers in England. Men, women, and children worked in dark factories for ten hours a day. Many of them became sick and died. At the same time, the rich people lived easy lives and didn't work.

Wells wanted to change things for the English worker. In *The Time Machine*, he wrote about a bad future that might come to pass if things didn't change. However, things did change for the better. We can hope that Wells's idea of the future isn't our future.

But Wells wrote about other things that did come true. He talked about a world war before we had one. He wrote about airplanes, tanks, and atomic bombs before we used them. When he died in 1946, he was called "the man who saw the future."

So far, no one has built a time machine. But, who knows? Maybe someday people will be able to travel to the future.

1 A Look at the Time Machine

The Time Traveler (we will call him that) was talking about deep matters. His usually pale face was bright. His eyes were shining as he spoke. Six of us were gathered at his house that night in 1895: a doctor, a very young man, a mayor, a psychologist, a storekeeper named Filby, and myself.

We were all good friends of the Time Traveler. Each of us admired his bright mind and his inventions. In fact, he had invented the chairs we sat on. We had eaten a very good dinner. And now, we were sitting around the table, making small talk. At least, I thought it was small talk. But it soon became plain that the Time Traveler was very serious. I had never seen him so excited.

"You must follow me carefully," he said, pointing a finger in the air. "Most of what you have learned in school about mathematics is wrong."

"Really," said Filby. "You ask a lot of us." (Filby liked to argue.)

"I don't ask you to believe anything without proof," said the Time Traveler. "And I can prove what I say. For instance: All things have shape and form. You can measure them by how high, wide, and deep they are. Right?"

"Of course," said the doctor. "We all know that."

"But you have left out time," said the Time Traveler. "It is the fourth way to measure things."

"I don't follow you," said the mayor.

"Let me put it this way," said the Time Traveler. "For something to be real to us, it has to be more than just wide, deep, and high. It has to last long enough in time for us to know that it's there."

"I don't understand," Filby said. "Either something is, or it isn't. Of course it lasts in time. Otherwise, it wouldn't be real. Time isn't the same as space."

"Ah, that's where you're wrong, Filby," said the Time Traveler. "Just because you can't travel in time, you think that nothing or no one *can* travel in time."

"This is really too deep for me," the mayor sighed.

"Not at all," said the Time Traveler. "It's all in how you look at it. Now, let's say you are a person in a cartoon in a newspaper. You can't cross over into the next box of the cartoon. But that doesn't mean it isn't there, does it?"

"I suppose not," said the doctor.

"Well, it's the same thing with time," the Time Traveler explained. "We think of time as something that can't be changed. What is past is gone forever. And we just have to wait for what is to come. In our own way, we are like the people in a cartoon. But just because we can't cross the lines doesn't mean that the past and the future aren't there. And I say these lines can be crossed."

"I think I see what you mean," the doctor said. "Things all have *four* dimensions: they are high, wide, deep, and exist in time. Time is like space. It's just another way to measure things. And it is just as real as the others."

"Now you have it!" cried the Time Traveler.

"But there is a difference," the doctor said, wagging his finger. "We can travel in space. We can go up, down, back, and forth. But we can't travel in time."

"Ah, but we can," said the Time Traveler, with a smile. "That's why I have called you all here tonight. I have been working for some years on this idea. I have invented a machine that will let me travel in time. At least, I have finished a small model of one. Now I will prove to you that it works."

"It can travel through time?" asked the young man. "What an idea!"

"It would be wonderful for history teachers," said the psychologist. "They could travel back and see what really happened."

"Well, what about the future?" said the young man. "You could put all your money in the bank to earn interest. Then you could travel years ahead and be rich."

"Well, if you ask me, this is all just small talk," Filby said. "You can't prove it."

"Oh, but I can," answered the Time Traveler.

"Prove it?" I said. "This I have to see!"

"And so you shall," said the Time Traveler.

"Of course, it's all a trick," Filby added.

"Trick or not, let's see it," said the mayor.

The Time Traveler smiled. Then he got up from the table and went out of the room. We heard him walk down the hall to his workshop. While he was gone, Filby started to tell us about a magician he once saw. But before he could finish his story, the Time Traveler came back.

The Time Traveler was holding something that was no bigger than the palm of his hand. It was about the size of a small clock. I have to admit it was well made—whatever it was. It had rods of bright metal. Some parts looked like glass, but they glowed without light shining on them. There were other things on it that I had never seen before.

"This is a small model of a machine I am building," explained the Time Traveler. He put the model on a small table near the fireplace. The only other thing on the table was an oil lamp. But there were many candles lit in the room. I could see everything clearly.

We all drew closer and looked carefully at the model. I think we were looking for some kind of trick. Because of this, I watched very closely. I was sure that with all of us watching, the Time Traveler could not trick us.

"Well?" said the psychologist.

"First of all, this is only a model of my machine," said the Time Traveler. But it *will* travel through Time. Look at this bar. It shines without any other light. It doesn't look quite real, does it?"

"It seems well made," said the doctor.

"It took me two years to make the model," said the Time Traveler. He pointed to the other parts of the machine. "When you press this white bar forward, the machine will go into the future. The other bar will send it into the past." He pointed to a seat on the model. "Here is where the time traveler will sit on the machine.

"In a minute, I will press the white bar. The machine will then disappear into the future. It will be gone forever. That's because there is no one on it to bring it back. Watch closely, now. I don't want to waste this model, and then have you tell me it was all a trick."

We were all quiet for a moment. The Time Traveler reached for the white bar. Then he

stopped. He turned to the psychologist and said, "No, I shouldn't do this. Here. Lend me your finger."

We watched the psychologist press the white bar with his finger. The machine began to glow. Then it began to blur. It seemed to spin. You could almost see through it, as if it were a ghost of a machine. Suddenly, it was gone! At the moment it disappeared, a candle near the fireplace was blown out. Now the small table was bare, except for the lamp.

The psychologist was the first of us to move. He looked under the table for the machine. I'm sure he thought it had been a trick. The Time Traveler laughed.

"Well, what do you think?" he asked.

"Do you mean to tell us that your machine is now in the future?" the doctor asked.

"That's right," answered the Time Traveler. He smiled. "What's more, I have nearly finished building a big machine. I plan to travel into time, myself."

"Hold on, now," said Filby. "It's one thing to show us a trick toy. It was good for some after-dinner fun. But tomorrow, in the daylight . . . That's another thing."

The Time Traveler smiled. "Would you like to see the Time Machine itself, then?" he asked. He stood up.

We followed him down the hall to his workshop. The machine was, indeed, a larger model of the one that had disappeared. But this one wasn't finished. The control bars weren't in place yet. I picked one up. Like the bar on the model, it was made of some kind of glass. It seemed to glow from the inside. On a table nearby, I saw some plans and drawings.

"All right," said the doctor. "We've seen it. Now stop joking with us. Do you mean to say that you're really going to travel through time on this thing? Or is this a trick—like the ghost you showed us last Christmas?"

"I have never been more serious in my life," said the Time Traveler. "I am going to travel into the future on this machine!"

None of us knew what to say. I looked at Filby. His face showed that he didn't believe a bit of it. He gave me a wink, too.

2 The Time Traveler Returns

I don't think that any of us believed in the Time Machine. Maybe it was because of the Time Traveler himself. He had a mind that was a bit too clever. You never knew when he was joking. If someone like Filby had told us a story like that, we would have believed him. In fact, *anyone* would believe Filby. He wasn't smart enough to lie.

But I have to admit that I thought about the Time Machine all that week. I couldn't get over the way the model had disappeared.

When I saw the doctor during the week, I mentioned the Time Machine model. He said that he once had seen something like it at a magic show. He was sure it had been a trick. But then I asked him how the trick was done. He didn't have a good answer for me.

The next Thursday, I was invited to dinner again at the Time Traveler's house. When I got there, I found four or five men already there. However, the Time Traveler wasn't there. The doctor was standing in front of the fire, looking at his watch. "It's half-past seven now," he said. "I suppose we should have dinner."

"Without our host?" I asked. "Where is he?"

"That's the funny thing," the doctor said. He showed me a note. "He left me this. He says that he'll be late. If he isn't here by seven, we should eat without him. He says he'll explain everything when he gets here."

"Well, it would be a shame to let dinner get cold," said a man who was a newspaper editor.

We sat down to eat. The doctor, the psychologist, and I were the only people who had been at the last dinner. Sitting next to the editor was a reporter. And next to him sat a quiet man with a beard.

As we ate, I talked a little about time travel. The others wanted to hear more. The psychologist explained what had happened the week before. He called it all a trick. He was still talking when I saw the door open. "At last he's here," I thought. The door opened wider, and the Time Traveler stood before us. I gave a cry of surprise.

"Good heavens!" cried the doctor. "What's wrong?" He also had seen the Time Traveler standing in the doorway. The others turned around to look.

The Time Traveler looked terrible. His coat was dusty and dirty. His clothes were torn. His hair was a mess, and his face was pale. He had a brown cut on his chin. It looked as if it were a few days old. He looked very tired and weak. For a moment, he just stood in the doorway. Then he came into

the room. He walked with a limp, as if his feet were sore from walking many miles.

He didn't say a word. He came toward the dinner table and pointed to the wine bottle. The editor gave him a glass of wine. He drank it down and gave us a weak smile.

"What in the world have you been doing, man?" asked the doctor. The Time Traveler didn't seem to hear him.

"Don't let me disturb you," he said in a weak voice. "I'm all right." He held out his glass again.

It was quickly filled for him. He drank it right down. "That's good," he said. Some of the color came back to his face. He looked around the room and at us.

"I'm going to wash up and put on fresh clothes," he said. "Please save me some meat, won't you? I'm starving for a bit of meat." The editor began to ask a question. The Time Traveler held up a hand. "I'll tell you soon enough. I'll be back in a few minutes."

As he left the room, I saw why he was limping. He had nothing on his feet but a pair of torn socks. And his feet were all bloody. Then the door closed behind him.

I could almost read the editor's mind. He was already making up a headline for his newspaper: *Famous Inventor Acts Strangely.*

"What's all this about?" asked the reporter. "What has our host been doing?"

I said that I was sure it had to do with the Time Machine. No one at the table took me seriously. All through the meal, the men made jokes. They were still laughing when the Time Traveler came back, dressed in clean clothes. He looked much better, but still very tired.

"Ah, there you are!" cried the editor. "I hear you've been time traveling into the middle of next week. So tell us, what's new?" He laughed. "Or should I say, what *will* be new?"

The Time Traveler didn't answer. He sat down at his place at the table. "Where's my dinner?" he asked. "Oh, I'm dying to eat some meat again!"

"Come on, tell us the story," said the reporter.

"Yes, don't keep us hanging like this," said the psychologist.

"I have to eat," said the Time Traveler. "I won't say a word until I have finished my dinner. Pass the salt, please."

At last, the Time Traveler pushed his empty plate away. "I'm sorry to have kept you waiting," he said. "But I was so hungry." He got up from the table. "Come into the other room," he said. "I have a long story to tell."

We followed him. Once we were seated, the Time Traveler looked at us. "I will tell you the whole story," he said. "But let me tell it in peace. Don't stop me for questions. I'm too tired to explain."

Everyone agreed not to break in on the Time Traveler. He began to tell his story. I have written it down. However, no matter how closely you read it, it won't explain everything. You had to be there. You had to see the man's face as he spoke. You had to see the faces of the other people. At first, they didn't believe him. As the story went on, they stopped smiling. After a time, no one looked at anything but the face of the Time Traveler. He told us this strange tale . . .

3 Time Traveling

"Last Thursday, I told some of you how the Time Machine worked. I even showed you the machine in my workshop. It's there now. But it is worn from travel. One of the control bars is cracked. The other bar is bent, but it still works.

"I thought I'd have all the work on it finished last Friday—the day after we had dinner. But at the last minute, I found that one of the bars was too short. I didn't get the machine working until this morning. The Time Machine began its career at ten o'clock today.

"I made some last-minute checks. Then I took my place on the seat. I took the control bars in my hands. I gave a small push on the forward bar.

"Right away, I became dizzy. I felt as if I were falling. I pressed the other bar to stop the machine. The feeling went away. I looked around me, at my workshop. It looked the same. Had anything happened? Then I looked at the clock. When I began, it had been ten o'clock. Now it was after four o'clock!

"Then I took a deep breath. I grabbed the bar, and off I went. The workshop faded, and then it grew dark. My housekeeper came into the workshop. She walked across the room, and didn't even see me. She moved so fast that she seemed to fly. I pushed the forward bar all the way.

"Night came so suddenly that it was like turning out a lamp. A new day came right after it. The changes came faster. Now I couldn't see my workshop at all. A buzzing sound filled my ears.

"I guess that at some time in the future, my workshop was destroyed. I suddenly found myself in the open air. I was going so fast that I couldn't follow moving things with my eyes. Even the slowest snail moved faster than a bullet! I went still faster.

"It's hard to tell you how it feels to travel in time. It isn't pleasant at all. You have the feeling that you're going too fast. You think that if you hit something, you'll die from the crash. I saw the sun hopping across the sky. Each minute became a day. And I went still faster.

"I saw trees growing so fast that they rose like puffs of smoke from the ground. I saw big buildings rise and fall in minutes. I kept going faster. After a while, I noticed that my speed was over a year a minute. I didn't want to stop.

"What wonderful things would I see? How far ahead of 1895 would the world be? Would there be no war, no sickness? I had high hopes. I pressed the bar to stop the machine. But I made the mistake of pushing it too hard.

"The machine was moving so fast that it stopped with a thud. I heard a sound like thunder. I was thrown headfirst into the air. When I landed, I think I passed out for a few seconds.

"When I came to, a heavy hail was falling. I was sitting on the ground. The machine was on its side next to me. The buzzing in my ears was gone. I looked around me. There were flowering bushes all around. The big purple and pink flowers were bending under the beating of the hail. In a moment, I was wet to the skin. I remember thinking, 'This isn't a very nice welcome for someone who has traveled so many years to see you.'

"After a while, I thought, 'What a fool I am to be getting wet like this. There must be some place I can go to get out of the rain and hail.' I looked around and saw a big white figure close to me. I looked up at it.

"It was very big. It looked like a lion with wings—like the sphinx in Egypt. But instead of the wings being folded back, they were spread out. I think the figure was made of marble. Its base was metal, which was green with age.

"The face of the sphinx was turned toward me. Its empty eyes seemed to watch me. There was a hint of a smile on its lips. It was very old and badly worn from the weather. I had the feeling that the sphinx was rotten inside—not from age, but from

a sickness. I don't know how long I stood there, looking up at it.

"The hail and rain began to let up. The sky was getting lighter. I began to think about this new age I was in. What would the people be like? Would they be like the people I knew? Or would they be so different that I would seem very strange to them? They might even kill me, thinking I was some dangerous animal!

"As the skies cleared, I saw large buildings nearby. They were white and shiny from the rain. The sun made them look even brighter. I felt afraid—afraid of what might come out of those buildings. I went to the Time Machine. After much hard work, I got it to stand up again.

"Once I was seated on the machine, I felt better. Now I could get away in a hurry, if I had to. I looked back at the big white buildings. High up on the wall of the nearest building, I saw a round opening. A group of people came out! They were wearing colorful robes. I could tell they had seen me.

"Then I heard voices coming toward me. Suddenly, I saw tiny people, running through the bushes. One of the men came out of the bushes.

"He was a small, thin creature—perhaps four feet high. He wore a short purple robe, with a belt at the waist. He had sandals on his feet. He didn't need to wear much more. For the first time, I noticed how warm the air was.

"He was beautiful and graceful. But he also looked weak, as if he could be broken easily. I relaxed, feeling that I was in no danger. I stood up and got off the Time Machine."

4 A New Kind of People

"In a minute, we were standing face to face. He came up to me and laughed. If he was afraid of me, he didn't show it. He turned to two others who were with him. He spoke to them in a strange language. I couldn't understand a word of it.

"Others came up. Soon, eight or ten of these little people were all around me. One of them tried to speak to me. I shook my head. Then I pointed to my ears and shook my head again. I was trying to tell them I didn't understand their language. One of them stepped forward. She touched my hand. Suddenly, I felt all their tiny hands upon my arms and back. I was uneasy for a second. Then it came to me what they were doing. They wanted to make sure I was real.

"I told myself, 'Why should I be afraid? I could pick the whole bunch up, and throw them around, if I wanted to.' But then I saw them also trying to touch the Time Machine. Quickly, I went to the machine. I took off the control bars, and put them in my pockets. I couldn't let these creatures fool with the machine. It was my only way of getting home. Then I turned back to the little people. I would try to get through to them somehow.

"I also took a closer look at them. Their faces were as fine as those of little dolls. They all had curly blond hair on their heads. But their faces and bodies were hairless. They had large, round eyes. In a way, they looked like deer, with their thin lips and pointed chins.

"What surprised me was the way they acted toward me. Here I was, a strange creature among them. But they didn't seem to want to know anything about me. No one tried to speak with me. They just stood around, smiling. Now and then, they spoke to each other. Their voices sounded more like birds cooing than people talking.

"I tried again to get through to them. First I pointed to the Time Machine, and then to myself. I stopped for a second. How could I explain the idea of time travel? I pointed to the sun. To my surprise, one of the little people did the same thing. Then he made a sound like thunder.

"I was surprised. The dial on the Time Machine said that I was in the year 802,701. I had always thought that the people of the future would be far ahead of the people of 1895. Were the people of the future fools? This little person was asking me a question that a child of 1895 wouldn't ask. He wanted to know if I had come from the sun, in a thunderstorm!

"I looked into his big eyes. I knew that I could never explain it to him. Instead, I nodded my head. Again, I pointed to the sun. I made the sound of thunder.

"They all took a few steps back and bowed to me. They probably thought I was some kind of god. They began to pick flowers and make them into chains. They put these chains around my neck. In a few minutes, I was almost covered with flowers.

"One of them took me by the hand. With the others following, we walked toward one of the big buildings I'd seen. As we walked by the big marble sphinx, it seemed to smile at me. I smiled back. What a joke! This was the world of the future. And its people were no smarter than five-year-olds! I didn't worry about the Time Machine being left alone. These people could never figure out how it worked.

"The building was bigger than I had thought. There were now hundreds of little people around me. But the building could have held thousands more. I looked closer at this great stone hall. Nobody took care of it. Little by little, it was falling apart.

"The floors were made of a shiny white metal. But as hard as the metal was, it showed signs of wear. It was as if thousands of little feet had worn it down. But how many thousands of years did it take?

"Small marble tables stood all around the hall. On these tables were piles of fruit. But what fruit! A strawberry was the size of a basketball, and an orange was bigger. The rest of the fruit was strange to me.

"The people made signs to me to sit down. Instead of chairs, we sat on pillows on the floor. They

began to eat right away. They threw the peels from the fruit into holes that were next to the tables. They ate more like animals than people. I joined in, but with better manners.

"As soon as I finished my meal, I tried again to talk to the little people. There had to be some way to reach them. I began by making little sounds. I made my voice go up, to mean I was asking a question. They thought I was funny. They saw me as a strange creature making noises. But I didn't let their laughing get to me. I kept at it.

"I felt like a schoolteacher in the middle of a crowd of children. But, little by little, I got through. In a few hours, I had learned some words. I knew how to say *you, me, her, him,* and even *hungry* and *eat.*

"But it was slow work. Like babies, they grew bored very quickly. They would wander off. I knew then that my 'lessons' would have to be short.

"There was another funny thing about them. They really were not interested in anything. I was something new to them. They kept coming up to me, just to get a good look. But once they did, they'd go off to find a new toy.

"I went out of the great hall to explore. I was surprised at how much things had changed. When I left my house in 1895, I was in the heart of London. The river was not far from my home.

"I went to the top of a large hill and looked around. There was no sign of the city. The only buildings were the ones close to me. The river had changed over the years. I could see that it had moved about a mile away from where it used to be. I walked back toward the great hall. I came across something that had been a large building. But now it was all junk. Flowers and grass grew over it.

"I noticed that something else was different. There were no small houses. Everyone lived to-gether in the buildings I saw when I arrived. They all ate together, and wore the same kind of clothes.

"And there was even more sameness. I hadn't noticed it before. I began to look closer at the little people. It was hard to tell which of them were men and which were women. I also couldn't tell if the children were boys or girls. They looked just like smaller models of their parents.

"I was full of wonder. So this was the world of the future. People were weak, but they didn't have to be strong. There was no heavy work to do. There were no wars to fight. Food grew all around. The people didn't have to plant the fruit, and they didn't have to pick it, except when they were hungry. With no work to be done, people had grown lazy. All they did was eat and play.

"I was seeing earth in the sunset of human history. It wasn't just that most of the buildings were in ruins. The minds of the people were the saddest ruins of all.

"Fewer people lived in that world than in our own time. But there was no war and no sickness. The people must have come up with a way to control their numbers. That way, there would be enough food and space for everyone.

"So I thought, then. But, as it turned out, I was wrong. I was very wrong—and in a way that is almost too awful to speak of!"

5 The Machine Disappears

"As I stood thinking, I looked around me. The sun had set. There was a bright full moon coming up. I looked down from the small hill I had climbed. I knew I would need to find a place to sleep.

"I tried to spot the big building where I had eaten dinner. I saw the sphinx. It got clearer as the moon grew brighter. I looked for the lawn I had landed on. Yes, I could see the flowering bushes. Then a chill came over me.

" 'No, that can't be the same lawn,' I said to myself. I looked again. But it *was* the same lawn. Suddenly, I was filled with fear. The Time Machine was gone!

"I ran down the hill. I fell a few times, and scratched my face. When I reached the lawn, the Time Machine was nowhere in sight. 'Maybe the little people put it in the bushes,' I thought. Like a crazy man, I began to look through the bushes. I searched through the bushes around the sphinx, but the machine wasn't there!

"I remember that I scared some kind of animal in the bushes. I didn't see it, but I heard it run

away. At the time, I thought it might be a deer. I learned later just what that animal was.

"I ran back to the big hall. The full moon lit my way. I burst into the room. All around me, the little people were sleeping on cushions on the floor.

"If they were surprised the first time they saw me, what must they have thought this time? I was cut, and my clothes were torn from beating the bushes. I cried out in a loud voice, 'Where is my Time Machine?' To see better in the dim light, I lit a match. This really scared them, and they jumped up. My heart sank inside me. They were afraid of the match. People had sunk so low that they had forgotten how to make fire!

"Suddenly, I couldn't bear to look at them. With a wild cry, I knocked several of them over. I ran outside again, into the moonlight. I went back to where the Time Machine had been. I must have looked around there for hours. Finally, I got so tired and felt so bad that I fell down on the lawn and slept.

"In the morning, I tried to get some help from the little people. They just weren't interested. It was hard to stop myself from hitting their smiling faces. I went from one to the other, trying to find out something—anything. But it was no use. I went back to the lawn where I'd slept. Then I saw something.

"There were deep tracks in the grass. Someone had dragged the Time Machine away. I followed the tracks. They led me to the base of the white sphinx. I looked up and saw that there were two big metal doors at the base of the sphinx. My Time Machine was inside the sphinx!

"I looked for a long time, trying to find some kind of doorknob or handle. I had to get inside. I had to find the Time Machine. But how did doors open in the year 802,701? Maybe the little people knew.

"I spotted one of them walking nearby. I grabbed his arm and led him toward the sphinx. He looked scared, and he ran away! I was used to the little people not caring about anything. But this fear was new. I tried asking others for help, but they all acted the same way. They were all frightened.

"Finally, I gave up trying to get their help. I went to the ruin of the big building, and took a big rock from it. I went to the metal base of the sphinx. I began to pound on it with the stone. I don't know how long I hammered.

"The metal was very old. Parts of it turned to dust under my blows. But I really didn't make a dent in it. In the end, I gave up. I went back to the big hall.

"Everything was different. It was as if I had some sickness and the little people were afraid of catching it. For two days, no one spoke to me. No one even came near me. I thought that maybe the sphinx was some kind of god to them. Maybe I had done a bad thing, hammering away at it. That's what I thought, anyway. I was to find out later how wrong I was.

"During the next few days, I took the chance to really look around. I climbed the highest hills I could find. Besides the buildings and the sphinx, only a few towers rose above the trees. They looked like big chimneys.

"I found another strange thing while I was walking around. There were deep, round holes in the ground. Low walls stood around them. At first, I thought they were water wells. But when I looked into one, I could not see a bottom. I dropped a rock into it. I didn't hear it hit bottom. There was no splash. I took a piece of paper from my pocket. I dropped it down. I thought it would go down slowly. But in a moment, it was sucked down, out of sight. I hung my head over the edge. From the darkness below, I heard a *thump-thump* sound. It was like the heartbeat of a huge animal. I wondered what was down in those holes.

"Other things bothered me. Where did the people's clothes come from? Everyone was well dressed. But there were no factories to make clothes. Where did their sandals come from? They were well made. But none of the little people I met could have made them. They didn't even know how to make fire! Who kept this world going?

"Then there was the question of my Time Machine. Someone or *something* had dragged it into the sphinx. Why? And what were those wells without water? What were those strange tall chimneys? What were they for? I felt I had clues. But it was all still a mystery. It was like finding a stone with words cut into it. Some of the words were in English. The rest might have been in Chinese. Then, on my third day in the year 802,701, my break came!

"On that day, I made a friend. A group of the little people were wading in a stream near the big buildings. One of them slipped on a rock. She was caught by the fast moving water.

"What happened next was hard to believe. No one tried to help her. No, it was worse than that. No one even paid attention. The poor creature was being carried away by the water. She was making little helpless cries. She might as well have been a rock or a tree. No one cared.

"When I saw that no one was going to help, I dived into the stream and pulled her out. She was cold, so I rubbed her hands and feet. In a few minutes, she came around. By now I had learned not to wait for a thank-you. I left her there.

"That happened in the morning. In the afternoon, I met her again. When she saw me, she began to smile. She greeted me in her odd language. She made a chain of flowers, and put it around my neck.

"In a few minutes, we were sitting and talking. I shouldn't say talking. We were mostly smiling and waving our hands. She kissed my hands. I

kissed hers. Using the few words I knew, I learned that her name was Weena. It was the beginning of an odd friendship that lasted for a week. It ended—as I will tell you!

"When I saved Weena, I didn't understand what I had gotten myself into. She followed me around like a puppy. Whenever I left her, she was upset. All she wanted to do was be near me. I began to look forward to seeing her, as well. Not that there was anything between us. She was like a young child. But I learned things from Weena.

"I learned that fear hadn't left this strange world. Oh, Weena was brave in the daylight. But she was awfully afraid of the dark. And it wasn't only Weena who felt that way. All the little people stayed in the big house after dark. They never slept alone.

"I was such a fool that I didn't learn from their fear. I kept sleeping outside."

6 The Morlocks and the Eloi

"One morning just before dawn, I woke up. It was that gray time of night—just before the sun comes up. It's then that your eyes can play tricks on you. I looked at the hills. I thought I saw ghosts! I looked again. I saw white ape-like creatures. They seemed to be carrying a dark body.

"I looked again, and they were gone. I rubbed my eyes. At the time, I felt that I had seen something important. But after the sun came up, I passed it off in my mind as a dream. I said nothing about it to Weena. I should have. I could have learned something. Instead, I had to learn the hard way.

"The next day was very hot. I had been walking around, trying to learn more about this future world. But the heat was too much for me. I spotted what looked like a cave. It seemed cool and dark, so I went inside.

"Suddenly, I froze. In the dark, I saw two red eyes watching me. I called out. I guess my voice didn't sound very brave. Then I reached out and touched something soft in the dark. The red eyes darted from side to side. Something ran past me. I turned and saw a strange ape-like figure run out

34

of the cave. It kept its head down in an odd way. It ran right into a big stone and fell down. Then the thing got up again, and ran into another cave.

"I didn't get a good look at it. It was white and had large reddish-gray eyes. Its white hair grew all the way down its back. I couldn't tell for sure if it walked on all fours. Maybe it just held its arms very low.

"Holding back my fear, I followed it. I went inside the other cave. There was no trace of the white thing. But I did find another one of those wells. Could the thing have gone down there?

"I lit a match and looked down the hole. I saw the thing. It was climbing down the sides of the hole. There were metal bars on the sides of the well. The thing was climbing down using these handholds. It looked like an evil white spider. I felt almost sick looking at it. Then my match burned out. All was darkness again.

"I don't know how long I stood there, thinking. Then, the truth came to me. Even though the creature I saw didn't look human, it was. In the future, there were two kinds of humans. The little people lived above ground. The white ape-like people lived below ground. I understood why the thing had run right into that big stone. From living underground for so many years, it was not used to light. That also explained why the thing had such big wide eyes. It was like a cat or an owl. Those eyes helped it to see in the dark.

"I started to think about why some people lived under the ground, while others lived in the sunshine above. It started back in our time—in 1895. Back then, many people worked in factories all day. They made the fancy clothes and things that the rich people could buy. But they spent all their time indoors and hardly ever saw the sun. They worked all their lives, just so that rich people could have a good time.

"It seemed clear to me. The little people wore clothes and sandals that the white things made. Instead of being thankful, the little people just enjoyed what the underground people did for them. They gave nothing, while the creatures underground lived like moles. I had a feeling that this world was like a beautiful ripe apple that had worms in the center.

"As best I could, I told Weena what I had seen. She didn't want to talk about it. However, she did tell me that the things living underground had a name. They were called Morlocks. For the first time, I also heard the name of the beautiful little people. They were called the Eloi.

"I was disgusted with the Eloi. What did they do to keep things going? Nothing! The poor Morlocks made this world run. And what did they get in return? An awful life, underground. Weena tried to tell me more about the Morlocks. But I didn't know enough of the Eloi language to understand what she said.

"I tried again to understand. I asked Weena more questions. She broke into tears. These were the first tears I had seen in this world. Weena was nice, and I couldn't stand to see her cry. I stopped asking her about the Morlocks. I lit a match for her. She liked that. I think she thought it was magic. In a few minutes, she was smiling and clapping her hands. And I was lighting one match after another."

7 Down in the Hole

"This may seem odd to you. For two days, I didn't have the nerve to follow up on what I had learned. I was put off by the ugly Morlocks. They were the color of worms and things that you see in jars in museums.

"In my heart I knew what I had to do. I had to go underground myself. It was the only way I would find my Time Machine.

"Instead, I continued to explore this new land. I walked for miles for two days. On the second day, I saw a big building far away. It was as big as the great hall of the Eloi. But it wasn't white. It was deep green. As I came closer to it, I saw that it was very shiny in the sunlight. What was it for? Were people in it?

"I wanted to go see the green building. But I knew that I was just putting off what I had to do. I had to go down one of those wells and look for my machine. I could go to the green building when I came back. I knew that I shouldn't waste any more time. Early the next morning, I headed for one of the wells.

"Weena came with me. At first, she was happy that we were out together for a walk. She didn't

know where I was going. She ran ahead of me, making happy noises. When I stopped at the mouth of the well, she got very upset. She didn't know what I was going to do. She was unhappy just being near the well.

"Good-bye, little Weena," I said. I picked her up and kissed her. Then I set her down. I leaned over the well, and began to feel for the handholds. I knew they were there. I had seen the Morlock use them. I had to go right away, before I lost my nerve.

"When Weena saw what I was doing, she went wild! She tried to stop me. She kept making sad little cries. I pushed her away, and began to climb down the well.

"I had to climb down about six hundred feet. The worst part of the climb was the handholds. They were made for a creature much smaller and lighter than I was. Once, one of the metal hand-holds gave way. For a few awful seconds, I hung by one hand in the dark. Then I felt lower, and found another metal grip.

"I stopped for a second and looked above me. The mouth of the well was now a small circle of blue. My arms and back hurt. I was so tired that I was afraid I would fall. Then I felt a hole in the wall. It seemed like some kind of tunnel.

"I swung myself into the hole. For a time, I just lay there, glad for the rest. The steady *thump-thump* noise was louder now. It was like the heart-beat of some strange animal that was moving closer.

"I don't know how long I lay there. Suddenly, something touched my face. I nearly jumped out of my skin. I lit a match. In the sudden light, I saw three creatures running away. They looked just like the Morlock I had seen the other day.

"They were all bent over, and pale like worms. Their eyes were huge, and seemed to have no lids. They weren't afraid of me in the dark. But the match scared them. They ran down the tunnel.

"I tried to call to them. But I guess they didn't speak the same language as the Eloi. Maybe they had gone to tell others that I was here. 'You're in for it now,' I said to myself.

"I kept moving along the tunnel. I didn't run into any more of the awful creatures. Soon the walls of the tunnel fell away. I felt I was in a very large room. The noise of the big machines was very loud now. I lit another match.

"I couldn't see much. A single match doesn't make that much light. But I could make out shapes. There were giant machines in the room. And there was a smell in the air. It was the smell of fresh blood! I looked around, and saw a metal table nearby. It had been set for a meal. I looked closer.

"I could see that, unlike the Eloi, the Morlocks ate meat. I wondered what kind of animals they ate. The piece of meat on the table was from a large animal. It was part of a leg bone. Just then, the match burned my fingers. I threw it down, and found myself in the dark again.

"I put my fingers inside the match box. I knew then that I was in trouble. I had only four matches left. I kicked myself for wasting them. When I came to this new land, I had a whole box full. The Eloi were so interested in matches that I had used them like toys. Now the only thing between me and the Morlocks was four matches!

"As I stood there in the dark, unseen hands began to grab and pull at me. I can't tell you how awful it felt. I could smell them, too. They had a dead meat smell that made me sick. I felt as if bugs were crawling all over me. Then I felt one of them reach for my box of matches!

"I gave a loud cry. The hands went away. I lit another match and set fire to a piece of paper from my pocket. I knew that it would last longer than a match would. I saw the Morlocks. There were gangs of them, hiding in corners from the light. But once the paper burned out, I could hear them. They were coming closer again.

"They weren't afraid of me anymore. I could hear them making noises as they came closer. I think that sound scared me more than anything else. They were laughing! I had to get out of there. I lit a match. Now I had only two left.

"When the Morlocks fell back from the light, I turned around and ran. I could hear them coming after me. I found the tunnel again. As fast as I could, I made for the well. I was running in the dark. I had to slow down. But the Morlocks could keep running. Those terrible creatures could see in the dark!

"I felt their hands grab me. I quickly lit my third match. I waved it in their faces. Up close, they looked even worse: those pale faces, with almost no chins, and those pink eyes with no lids. I wasted no time. I turned and ran again.

"I made it to the place where I had climbed down. They were close behind me. I was trying to find the handholds when they grabbed me. I nearly died of fear. I took out my last match, just as hands grabbed my legs. I was being dragged back to the tunnel! Somehow I lit my last match.

"But I had forgotten something. It was windy inside the well. And the same wind that blew inside the well blew out my match. I had one hand on a handhold. A Morlock had hold of my foot. Somehow, I pulled myself up.

"The Morlock wouldn't let go. I prayed that the handhold wouldn't come out of the wall. I pulled up hard, kicking wildly. My shoe fell off my foot. I was free! I climbed quickly, like a monkey. I could hear one of the Morlocks right below me! I climbed faster. When I reached the top, the Morlock gave up. The bright light of the sun stopped him.

"I crawled over the edge of the well, and fell onto the ground. I think I passed out. When I came to, Weena was kissing my face. She was making little cries of joy. I guess she had thought she would never see me alive again. I shook inside. She had almost been right!"

8 The Green Palace

"Now I knew I was in trouble. My machine was below ground. So were the Morlocks. To make things worse, I had no more matches. I had nothing to use to scare the Morlocks, and I had no weapon to fight them. Each night, the moon was getting smaller. Soon there would be a night without a moon. On that night, the Morlocks would come out of their holes, like evil white worms.

"What was I to do? How could I keep the Morlocks away? And, most important, how could I get my Time Machine back? There had to be an answer, somewhere.

"Then I thought about the big green building. I already had given it a name in my mind: the Green Palace. It was one place I had wanted to explore. Maybe it could give me some answers. I set off toward it the next day.

"Weena went with me. As before, she seemed excited and happy. She must have thought that our journey was another game. I felt like a parent taking a child for a walk. As we walked, Weena picked flowers. Then she put them in my pockets. I don't think she had ever seen pockets. The Eloi had none in their robes. She decided that pockets were the perfect place to keep flowers."

The Time Traveler smiled sadly. He looked at his guests seated around him. He reached into one of his pockets. He took out two dried white flowers. He put them on the table before him.

We gathered around to look at them. I knew that I had never seen flowers like those. We began to talk about the flowers. But the Time Traveler stopped us, with a wave of his hand. Then he went on with his story.

"We spent the day walking. When it got dark, I found a spot under a tree. I slept sitting up, with my back to the tree. I knew that no one could come up behind me that way. Weena slept with her head leaning on my arm. I didn't sleep much. There was a very small moon. From time to time, I heard something moving. But I didn't see any Morlocks.

"It was late the next afternoon when we got to the Green Palace. Weena and I walked inside. We found ourselves in a very large room. In the middle of the room, I saw something that filled me with joy. It was a skeleton of a dinosaur. The Green Palace was a museum of some kind! I hoped that I could find things to help me. Maybe I could find out what the Morlocks really were and why they lived under the ground.

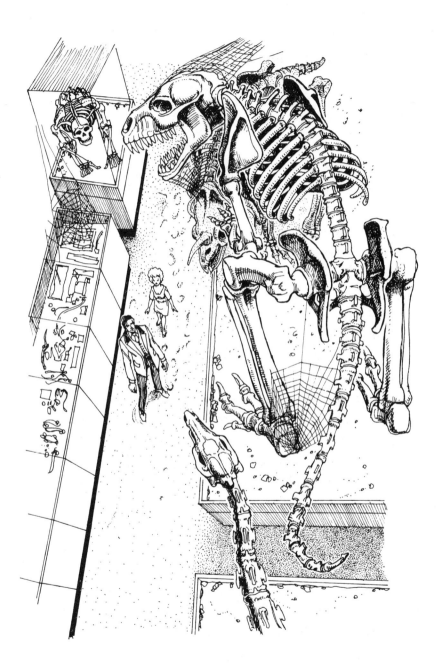

"We left the dinosaur hall. The next room was filled with different kinds of rocks and minerals. This gave me hope. If they had all kinds of minerals, they might have sulfur. And with sulfur, I could make matches. But I had no luck. Sadly, I walked on.

"The next room was full of machines. I knew some of them right away. Others were strange to me. Even the ones that were new to me were very old. Most of the machines were rusty and falling apart. Then I got an idea. I saw a large machine with a big iron handle on it. I climbed onto the machine and took hold of the handle. I pulled hard. The piece of iron came off in my hand. It was about three feet long.

"I lifted the iron bar and swung it. It was just right for my needs. I could use it as a club. Now I had something to fight the Morlocks with!

"In the next room, I found something wonderful. There it was, inside a glass case: a box of matches! I broke the glass with my iron bar. My hands were shaking as I picked up the box. My common sense told me that the matches wouldn't work. I was sure that they were too old. But I kept hoping. I took out a match and rubbed it on the rough side of the box. It lit!

"I let out a shout of joy. It scared poor Weena. But I didn't care. Now I had two things to use against the Morlocks: an iron club and fire. As I walked into another room, I felt much better. I was feeling more sure of myself now.

"What I found next was beyond my dreams. Inside a glass case, looking brand-new, were two sticks of dynamite. This was wonderful. The matches still worked. Maybe the dynamite would, too. I almost laughed out loud. I had planned to use my iron bar to open the doors to the sphinx. But with dynamite, I could blow the doors apart. I took Weena's hand and led her outside the Green Palace.

"I told her to stay where she was. I took one of the dynamite sticks and walked to a safe distance. I took a match and lit the fuse to the dynamite. Then I ran back to where Weena was. I waited for the dynamite to go off. But it never did.

"I went back to where I had put the dynamite. I picked up the stick. Then I looked closer. Of course it didn't work. It was a fake. It had to be. No one would put real dynamite in a museum. When real dynamite gets old, it becomes very dangerous. A small tap can set it off.

"Weena and I went back into the Green Palace. I finally found some guns. But they were all rusty, and wouldn't work. Then I found some other guns that were still shiny. But there were no bullets for them.

"I spent the next few hours going through the museum. I did find some books. But when I touched them, they fell to dust. My last chance to find out about the Morlocks and the Eloi was gone.

"I looked sadly at the pile of dust. This was all that was left of thousands of years of learning. I knew that the Eloi could not read. Maybe that was the saddest part of all.

"I kept on walking through the museum. In one room, I found a jar with some white lumps in it. I took the cover off the jar. Right away, I could tell what was in it. You can't mistake the smell of camphor. Camphor is used to keep moths out of closets. But it also burns easily and brightly. What I had found was almost a firebomb. I put the jar in my pocket.

"Then I noticed that it was getting dark outside. I also noticed the floor under my feet. Like the floor in the Eloi's hall, it was made of white metal. But all the other floors in the Green Palace were dusty. This floor was clean. Someone used this floor all the time. That could only mean one thing: Morlocks.

"Quickly, I took Weena outside. I wasn't afraid. After all, I could fight the Morlocks. I had fire. I had a club. But I knew that we had to get out of there. There was no reason to look for a fight. And I didn't want us to get trapped inside the Green Palace.

"The sun was almost down when we set out for the Eloi's hall. I knew that we couldn't make it

without stopping to sleep. As we walked, I began to pick up dry sticks. Weena saw me picking up the sticks. She thought it was a new game. She began to gather sticks and bring them to me.

"Soon I had a big bundle of sticks under one arm. I held my iron club in that hand. The other hand had to stay free. With a club, matches, and camphor, I felt safe. I knew what to do if I met a Morlock.

"I thought about what I had seen underground. I decided to stop lying to myself about the Morlocks. I wouldn't let myself think the truth before. But now I knew what the Morlocks were.

"I laughed at how foolish I had been. I had thought of them as 'the poor Morlocks.' I had thought that they worked so hard for the Eloi. How could I have been so wrong?

"Yes, the Morlocks made clothes and sandals for the Eloi. But the reason made me sick. They cared for the Eloi. Just as we cared for our cattle in 1895. They wanted the Eloi to be healthy, so the Morlocks could kill them—and eat them!

"I held the iron bar tightly. It was never in me to kill anyone. The idea had always made me sick. But killing a Morlock would be different. They weren't human. Maybe they had been like us once. But now they were the lowest things on earth. They were cannibals. They ate human flesh. I knew that if I came across a Morlock, I would kill it on the spot."

9 Surrounded by Morlocks

"As I thought of Morlocks, I kept walking. It began to get very dark. It was hard to see the ground.

"Suddenly, I heard a sound in the bushes behind us. Weena heard it, too. She gave a small cry of fear. We walked faster. The sound followed us. I knew what it was: the Morlocks. We had been seen at the Green Palace. Now that the daylight was gone, they were coming after us.

"I soon saw that Weena couldn't keep up with me. My legs were much longer than hers. But I couldn't carry her. I had sticks under one arm, and the iron club was in my other hand. I stopped, and dropped the sticks. I knew what to do. Weena was scared. She wanted to keep going. I smiled and said soft words to her. I wasn't afraid.

"I opened the jar of camphor and took out one lump. I put it on my pile of sticks. Then I put the jar back in my pocket. I took out a match and lit it. I dropped the match on the camphor. It burst into flames right away. Behind us, I heard sounds in the bushes. The Morlocks were running away. 'Let them try to follow us now,' I thought.

"I grabbed Weena's hand just in time. She had never seen a roaring fire before. She was about to put her hand in it. Maybe she thought it was a new toy. I pulled her away, and we began walking again.

"I kept thinking about how sad this was. In this future age, half of the people were cannibals. And the other half didn't even know what fire was.

"We walked on for about half an hour. Then I heard the sounds again. But this time, they weren't coming from behind us. Suddenly, I understood what was happening. What a fool I had been! The Morlocks weren't just behind us. They were all around us. They were making a big circle and closing in on us. I could have kicked myself. If Weena and I had stayed near the fire, we would have been safe. But we had walked away from it. Now the Morlocks had cut us off. In a second, I felt cold Morlock hands on me. Weena screamed.

"I swung my iron bar. I hit something in the dark. I heard an awful cry—the sound of a hurt Morlock. I swung again. I wanted to light a match. But I would have to let go of my club to do it. Weena screamed again. I called out her name. There was no answer. I heard the Morlocks closing in. They were making their awful laughing sound.

"I took the chance, and dropped my club. As fast as I could, I went for my matches. But the second I let go of the club, they were on me. I felt those cold hands, and I smelled that odor of blood. I thought I was going to be sick. Somehow, I lit a match.

"In the match light, I saw the Morlocks. There were hundreds of them around us! They ran from the light. I saw Weena a few feet away. She was lying on the ground. She wasn't moving. The match went out. I lit another. I couldn't keep this up all night. I would run out of matches. Then the Morlocks would be on us again.

"I looked at the dry grass under my feet. I took out the jar of camphor. I emptied it onto the dry grass. I dropped the match on it. It burst into flame. I ran to Weena, and pulled her close to the fire. Then I pulled down branches from the trees. They were green, but the camphor made them burn. It worked. The Morlocks were staying away.

"I tried to wake Weena. But I couldn't. I could tell that she wasn't dead. But she didn't answer me. She didn't even open her eyes. I moved her closer to the fire. I got more branches and fed the flames. Then I sat down to wait for sunrise.

"I woke up to find hands all over me. The fire was out! I reached for my club. It was gone. I went for my matches. They were gone, too. I felt hands grab my hair. I was being dragged away. I swung wildly in the dark, and hit a Morlock. One of my arms was now free. As I tried to free the other arm, my hand found something hard on the ground. The iron bar!

"I let out a cry of anger. I swung the bar. It hit something, and I heard a terrible cry of pain. I swung the bar again and again. In a few minutes, I was on my feet. I stood against a tree trunk and kept swinging the bar. But the Morlocks kept coming. How long could I last? My arms were getting tired. The bar was getting heavy. And still the Morlocks came at me.

"I saw one running straight at me. I hit him with the bar. He dropped like a stone. Suddenly I stopped. How was I able to see that Morlock coming at me? Were my eyes getting used to the dark? I looked and saw an orange glow in the sky. Was it sunrise already? No, it couldn't be. The glow was . . .

"Then, I knew. It was the light from the first fire I had started. It didn't rain much in this world. The trees and grass were dry. I had started a forest fire back there! This time, the Morlocks weren't running to get me. They were running to get away from the fire.

"I could see clearly now. I swung the iron bar at a passing Morlock. It fell to the ground. The creature hadn't even seen me. Even the dim light of the fire was too bright for the Morlocks. The light made them blind.

"I made my way to the top of a small hill. I looked down. The forest fire was getting bigger. It was being spread by the wind. It was forming a

circle. The Morlocks were now cut off from the Green Palace.

"They were going crazy. I saw some of them run right into the fire. Morlocks were running and screaming all around me. I had to move fast, or the flames would catch me, too.

"I began running in the direction of the Eloi's home. I kept calling Weena's name. I looked all around. She was gone. The Morlocks had gotten her. The fire was getting closer and closer. I couldn't stay to look for Weena any more.

"Fewer Morlocks were in my path now. But I killed any that I saw. They had taken little Weena. Soon, there were no Morlocks. Half out of my mind, I ran on. The sun came up, and I still ran.

"Finally, I came to the land of the Eloi. I stopped at the spot where I had stopped my Time Machine. I could see the white sphinx. I fell down on the soft grass. I felt as if I could sleep forever.

"I woke up in the late afternoon. Among the Eloi, life went on as usual. No one cared that I had come back. Maybe they never knew I had gone. The Eloi played, sang, and danced. They still played in the stream where I had saved Weena. Seeing the stream made my heart heavy. Weena was gone forever.

"One thing made me feel better. Weena probably had felt no pain. She had passed out. She may have died in the fire. But many Morlocks had died, too. I took the iron bar and walked toward the sphinx. I put my hand in my pocket, and took out the flowers I showed you. I felt like crying.

"But when I put the flowers back in my pocket, I felt something else in there. I still had a few loose matches! The Morlocks had stolen the box, but some matches had fallen out. A smile came to my lips. I had the iron bar. I had matches. I continued to walk toward the sphinx. I almost hoped to see a Morlock.

"I was going to use the iron bar to pry open the big doors. But when I got to the sphinx, I couldn't believe my eyes. The doors were already wide open. And inside, in the shadows, I could see the shape of my Time Machine!"

10 The End of Our World

"I stopped for a second, almost afraid to go inside. Then I reached into my pockets. I still had the control bars to the Time Machine. I smiled. After all my trouble, the doors were open. I dropped the iron bar on the ground. In a way, I was sorry that I wouldn't need it. My memory of the Morlocks was still strong.

"The Time Machine was on a raised platform. I looked it over. It was in perfect shape. It had even been cleaned and oiled. Loose screws had been tightened. It was the Morlock mind at work. For many years, they had taken care of underground machinery. To them, any piece of machinery had to be cleaned and oiled.

"As I walked up to the machine, a thought came into my mind. I knew why the doors to the sphinx were open. I knew what the Morlocks were up to. I understood how their minds worked. I could have laughed out loud.

"I put one of the control bars in place. Just then, the doors shut with a clang. I was now in darkness. It was just as I thought. The Morlocks were trying to trap me. They couldn't get me before.

Now they thought they had me. They thought that they had taken all my matches.

"I could hear them coming in the dark. I heard their laughing sound. I could have laughed, myself. In a second, I would light a match. Then I would put the other control bar in the machine. I would push one of the bars, and disappear. There was a smile on my lips as I reached for a match.

"It wouldn't light! I had made a mistake. These matches could light only on the side of the box. And the Morlocks had taken the box! In a second, the Morlocks were on me. I swung my fist. I got one of them.

"I had to get the second bar in place. But I couldn't see in the dark. A hand grabbed the control bar. I swung my head toward that cold hand. The Morlock and I bumped heads. It hurt me. But the Morlock let go of the control bar.

"I screwed the bar in place. I got onto the seat of the Time Machine. Another set of hands pulled at me. I pushed the Morlock off the machine. I was now half on and half off the machine. Somehow, I got to the control bars. I pushed forward as hard as I could. In a second, I was gone.

"I have already told you how time travel feels. It makes you dizzy. And that's when you are sitting straight up. But this time, I was half off the machine. It began to spin. I had to hang on. If I fell, I would be lost. I don't know how long I hung on for my life. Finally, I got myself straight on the seat.

"I looked at the dials. I saw that I'd made a mistake in the dark. I wanted to go back to 1895. But I had set the machine to go forward in time. And I was going faster and faster. The dials showed that I was traveling millions of years into the future.

"Suddenly, I could see the sky. The sphinx was gone from around me—turned to dust by the years. I began to slow down the machine. I didn't want to stop too quickly. That's what happened the last time.

"When the machine stopped, I looked around me. Was this the same earth? I had landed on an empty beach. The sands seemed to go on forever. A bright red sun beat down. There were no clouds in the sky. But what was the sea doing here? Where was the land of the Eloi? All that once was London was now under water. Over millions of years, the sea was taking back the land. Then, far away, I saw something move.

"It was too far to see clearly. The thing was moving slowly. I watched as it came closer. Then I saw what it was. It was a huge crab. It was the size of a dinner table. I could see its claws now. One of them could cut a person in half.

"I saw the feelers moving. I looked at its big eyes. The creature's mouth was the worst part. It

was slimy, and had things moving inside it. I felt sick as I watched it.

"Just then, I felt something tickle my face. It was sticky, like a spider web. I brushed my face with my hand. I turned around. It wasn't a spider web. Right behind me was another huge crab. What I felt were the things inside its mouth! I screamed, and pushed the control bars of the Time Machine. In a second, the ugly thing was gone.

"As I traveled farther into the future, a strange thing happened. The sun stopped moving across the sky. It stayed in one place, far away. The moon was never in the sky.

"I stopped the Time Machine, and looked around. The planet seemed dead. It was very cold, and snow was falling around me. Nothing moved. I heard no sounds.

"Suddenly, I knew why. The earth had stopped turning. It still went around the sun. But half of the earth was in darkness all the time. It never got light or warm.

"This, then, was it—the end of it all. All of our dreams and our history were gone. The earth was a huge chunk of rock without life. Sadly, I set the controls of the Time Machine for the year 1895."

11 The Time Traveler's Return

"So I started to come back. I was so tired that I fell asleep as I sat on the machine. As I slept, millions of years flew by.

"When I awoke, the days and nights had returned. The planet was turning again. I went faster. I saw mountains rise from piles of dust. I even saw big trees grow small, and zip into the ground. I saw buildings disappear, from the top downward. I was in the age of people again.

"I slowed down the machine. Once more, the walls of my workshop were around me. I was getting closer to my own time. Then I saw my housekeeper.

"Do you remember how she shot across the room the first time? Now she was moving backward. But she walked so slowly that a snail could have passed her! Finally, she backed out the workshop door. The door closed.

"I brought the machine to a stop. I looked at the dials. I was back where I'd started. It was tonight—Friday evening. I had been gone for eight days. I had traveled millions of years. Yet, here it was the same day I had left!

"I looked around my workshop. Everything was the same. Or was it? My machine was now much closer to the far wall. What had happened? Then I knew. The Morlocks had moved the machine. When I had stopped in the land of the Eloi, I was about ten feet away from the sphinx. Now, I was ten feet closer to the wall. Far in the future, part of my workshop would be inside the sphinx.

"I got off the machine. As my feet touched the floor, I felt a stab of pain. I looked down at my feet. My shoes were gone. I had lost one to a Morlock in the well that day. I had taken off the other one so I could walk. I saw that my feet were bloody.

"I was a mess. My face and hands were full of cuts. My clothes were torn. I was covered with dirt. I left my workshop, and walked down the hall.

"I was passing the dining room door, when I heard you all inside. I smelled the dinner. Suddenly, I was very hungry. I hadn't eaten for over two days. And before that, I had only fruit to eat. The smell of the roast beef got to me. I had to eat.

"I know I must have looked awful when I came into the dining room. But you know the rest of the story. I washed. I changed clothes, and I ate. And now, I have told you my story."

The Time Traveler looked at us. After a time, he said, "I know that you won't believe all this." He looked at the doctor. "Take it as a lie, then—or as a sign of things to come. Say I dreamed it all, in my workshop. Say it's a story that I made up. But, as a story, what do you think of it?"

He picked up his pipe. He tapped it, and then filled it. For a long while, no one said anything. I think we all were nervous. What can you say to someone who tells a tale like that? I looked at the others.

I saw the way the doctor looked at the Time Traveler. It was plain that he thought the man was crazy. The editor cleared his throat. He took out his watch and checked the time. He stood up and said, "What a shame you don't write stories for a living." He put his hand on the Time Traveler's shoulder.

"You don't believe me?" the Time Traveler asked.

"Well . . ."

"I thought not," said the Time Traveler. He turned to us. "Where are the matches?" he asked. He lit one, and spoke as he puffed on his pipe. "To tell you the truth, I hardly believe it myself. And yet . . ."

He looked at the white flowers on the table. Then he looked back at us. It was as if he were saying, "What about those flowers? Did I dream them, too?" The doctor came over to the table.

He picked up one of the flowers. He looked at it closely.

"I've never seen a flower like it," the doctor said.

His words seemed to shake up the others. The doctor was an expert on flowers. We all knew that. If the flowers were real, what about the rest of the Time Traveler's story? Was it true, too? The editor looked at his watch again.

"Say, it's almost one o'clock," he said. "How will we get home?"

"There are plenty of cabs at the railroad station," said the reporter. "We can get one there."

The doctor was still looking at the white flowers. "Odd," he said. "I just can't place these flowers. May I take them? I want to study them."

"Certainly not," said the Time Traveler.

"Then tell me this. Where did you *really* get them?" the doctor asked.

"I told you," the Time Traveler answered. "Weena put them in my pocket."

Suddenly, he put a hand to his head. He looked pale. I thought he was going to pass out. Then he spoke. "I think it's all going," he said. "I'm back home now. And it all seems like a dream to me. Was it real? Did I really travel through time?

"You all are so real. It makes me wonder. Did I ever build a Time Machine? Or was it all a dream? I must know!"

Saying this, he picked up the table lamp. He walked down the hall to his workshop. We all got up and followed him. In the lamplight, we saw his Time Machine. Yes, it was bent in places. But it was still wonderful to see.

Seeing the machine seemed to make the Time Traveler feel better. He smiled weakly and said to us, "It's all right now. The story I told you was true. Forgive me. I'm sorry I brought you out here. It's cold here in the workshop."

He led us back to the heated part of the house. We all began to put on our coats. It was time to leave. One by one, we said goodnight to our host. Before he left, the doctor told the Time Traveler that he was "suffering from overwork." The Time Traveler laughed.

I rode in a cab with the editor. We talked about the story we'd heard. The editor didn't believe a word of it. He said it was all "a fancy lie." I didn't say anything to that. But the story stayed on my mind. I wanted to see the Time Traveler again. I wanted to talk to him about it.

The next day, I went to the Time Traveler's house. His housekeeper opened the door. She told me that he was in his workshop. I said I'd go there alone. I knew the way.

But the Time Traveler wasn't there. The Time Machine was there, in the middle of the room. I put a hand on one of the control bars. The machine began to shake. I felt dizzy. Scared, I took my hand away. I looked around. I was afraid that someone had seen me touch the machine. I felt like a small child in a room he wasn't supposed to see.

I left the room. I was walking down the hall when I saw the Time Traveler. He had a big sack in one hand, and a camera in the other. He smiled.

He told me that he'd like to talk to me, but couldn't at that moment.

"I'm very busy with my Time Machine," he said.

"Then it's real?" I asked. "You *can* travel in time?"

"Really and truly," he said. "In fact, give me half an hour. I'll prove it to you. I'll have things to show you—and pictures, too. Just go into the living room and sit down. Read the newspaper." Then he went into his workshop, and closed the door.

I went into the living room. I sat down and began reading. A few minutes later, I thought of something. I had forgotten that I had a date with a friend. I couldn't wait here. But I didn't want to leave without telling the Time Traveler. I got up and walked back to his workshop.

When I got to the door of the room, I heard sounds inside. I heard the Time Traveler start to say something. Then his voice stopped. It was as if his voice had been cut off. As I opened the workshop door, I heard the sound of breaking glass. I rushed inside.

In the center of the room, I saw what looked like a ghost of the Time Machine. You could see right through it. I also saw the ghost of someone on it. Then, suddenly, it was gone! The room was empty.

Just then, the Time Traveler's housekeeper came into the room. We didn't say a word. We just

looked at each other. After a few seconds, we began to speak.

"Has he gone out your way?" I asked.

"No, sir," she said. "No one has come out this
way. I thought I would find him in here."

We stood around and waited. I was hoping that
the Time Traveler would come back soon. He
would have proof. He would have pictures. But he
didn't come back. Now I'm afraid I must wait a
lifetime. The Time Traveler disappeared three
years ago. And, as everyone knows, he has never
returned.

But I can't help wondering. Will he ever come back? Which way in time did he go this time? Is he back in the days of the cave dwellers? Or did he go back millions of years, to the age of dinosaurs?

Or maybe he went into the future again. Maybe this time, he went to a better age. To an age where people work and live together happily. Where there is no killing or sickness. And there are no bad creatures like the Morlocks. I hate to think that the future must be the way it was in the story I heard. Maybe the Time Traveler can change the future. I hope so. I have hope for the future of humankind.

But I will never know the future. I can only live my own life, and hope that things will get better— hope that the future will bring a world of peace and beauty.

I still have two strange white flowers. They are all dried up now. But they have taught me something. Even in the land of the Eloi, when people's minds and strength were gone, tenderness remained. Weena's simple gift of flowers showed that even with everything in ruins, tenderness remained. Call it love, if you will. I think it is the one real hope we all have.